Understanding Christianity —What It Means to Become a Christian

Brent Devenney

Understanding Christianity —What It Means to Become a Christian

1st Edition (Rev.07): March, 2013

ISBN: 978-1-300-50382-8

Contact: Pastor Brent Devenney, daybreakvermont.org

Book available at:
http://www.lulu.com/spotlight/BrentDevenney

ePublisher: Lulu Enterprises, Inc. (lulu.com)
3101 Hillsborough Street, Raleigh, NC 27607

RELIGION / General
A description of Christian conversion

Book jacket artwork, design, and photography by Shaun Stotyn.
Additional photography by Cullen Schill.
Formatting, editing, and feedback by Daybreak Community Church members and by Wayne Lavitt.

CONTENTS

Preface

I wish I could say that talking to others about my Christian faith always comes naturally and easily for me, but I cannot. Because of this I am often guilty of not doing it or when I do it – it doesn't go the way I wanted. In hindsight, many times I wish I had said this or that. That is why I am writing this book. I want something I can hand off to my friends, family members, colleagues, and acquaintances to help make Christianity and becoming a Christian understandable. Perhaps in a book I can cover those things I wish I had said. My hope and prayer for this undertaking is that after you read it Christianity makes sense to you. My hope and prayer is also that others will find this to be a useful book to give to their loved ones, friends, colleagues, and acquaintances.

Believe it or not, I have found many people, even the church going type, do not have a good understanding of Christianity. Perhaps the most common misconception people have about

Christianity is that it is about following rules and being good or religious. The opposite is really what Christianity is about. Christ came because we can't be good enough or religious enough. This really is what distinguishes Christianity from most other religions. In most other religions, it is about obeying God so we are accepted by Him. In Christianity, it is about obeying him because **we have been completely accepted by Him** through Christ. Said another way, Christianity really isn't about a religion, it is about a relationship. I hope in these next pages to explain how one enters into this relationship.

In the Bible, God speaking through the prophet Jeremiah says "If you seek me you will find me when you seek me with all of your heart." I don't want to start off on the wrong foot, but I do have a bit of a challenge for you if you are not certain you are a follower of Christ. I am hoping that before you begin reading this book you will say a prayer. I am hoping that you will pray "with all of your heart" that God will reveal Himself to you. I believe that if you pray this prayer God will certainly answer it by revealing Himself to you. It's one of those prayers that comes with a guaranteed Yes! May

God bless you and speak to you as you read
these pages.

Prayerfully,

Brent

1. "See You Later"

For the past twenty years or so I have worked simultaneously as a pastor and an oncology (cancer) nurse. I like to say "half jokingly" that these two professions have benefited my introverted personality especially when riding public transportation like planes or buses. When the person beside me initiates a conversation with the question "What do you do for a living?" and I reply with "I am a cancer nurse." or "I am a pastor." it is usually a conversation stopper. Who wants to talk about cancer or worse yet – talk to a preacher. So due to these two jobs, I encounter a lot less conversation and get a lot more reading done when I am on a plane or bus.

One of the reasons that this stops the conversation is that most people equate cancer with dying. Fortunately, now-a-days, cancer is more often cured than not, however, I have seen many lose their battle to cancer. As a nurse and a pastor, I have been at the bedside of many people who have crossed over into eternity as their battle with cancer has ended.

Perhaps the most dramatic eternal cross-over that I have witnessed was the death of my friend Harriett McClean. I met Harriett when I was working as an oncology nurse at a hospital in north Louisiana. Harriet had Stage 4 ovarian cancer and was in and out of the hospital many times towards the end of her life. During that time our relationship evolved from a nurse/patient relationship to one of friendship. I was a fairly new Christian at the time and she also was a follower of Christ. We had many good conversations about our mutual faith in Christ.

The last time she was hospitalized, Harriett was taking her nightly pills and unfortunately, choked on them. It became an emergent situation quickly and Harriett ended up being put on a ventilator (breathing machine). Several days later it became obvious that she would not tolerate coming off the ventilator without placing a tracheostomy for her to breathe. Even though Harriett was on the ventilator, she was still conscious and able to communicate by writing. She communicated that she did not want a tracheostomy or to continue to be hooked up to a ventilator. She wanted an opportunity to say goodbye to her family and friends and then be taken off the ventilator allowing for a natural death. Eventually, the opportunity came for me to say my goodbye to Harriett. I had the opportunity to tell her that I loved her and appreciated all of her conversations and friendship. In writing she also communicated her love for me and appreciation for our friendship. I will never forget that conversation and especially the look of peace that she had on her face as she was facing her imminent death. But the thing I will remember the most is what happened when I turned to leave, she grabbed my arm and began to write down something else. After writing a few words she turned them towards me so I could see them. Three words I will never forget "See You Later." Those three words along with her peaceful countenance, are forever etched in my memory.

I believe those three words capture the essence of the Christian faith. I don't mean to suggest that the Christian faith is only good for the ever-after, Jesus also came to give us life in the here and now (John 10:10). However the key to life in the here and now from a biblical perspective starts by making certain of our ever-after. Paul, the apostle who God used to write much of the New Testament said it this way "For to me, living means living for Christ, and dying is even better" (Philippians 1:21 NLT). A person really can know that when they die they are going to Heaven. Christ came "so that we may know we have eternal life" (1 John 5:13 ESV).

The way a person knows they are going to Heaven is really twofold. First they can know because they have done the two essentials required to enter into a relationship with Christ. Those two essentials are what the Bible calls repentance and faith. Paul summed up what it means to become a Christian when he said that he went about publicly and privately teaching "repentance toward God and faith in our Lord Jesus Christ." **I like to sum up repentance and faith as having Christ as your Forgiver and Leader.** Secondly you can know you are going to Heaven because you have experienced the change that comes along with becoming a Christian. "If anyone is in Christ," the Bible says "the new creation has come: the old has gone, the new is here!" (2 Corinthians 5:17

NIV). The Bible attributes this change to the Holy Spirit taking up residence in a person's heart (Ephesians 1:7).

In chapter three and four we will be looking at in more detail at the two essentials (repentance and faith) needed for a relationship with Christ. In chapter five we will be looking at the change that happens to a person when one sincerely responds to God with repentance and faith. But, first we must understand why we need Christ and that is the goal of chapter two.

2. Our Greatest Need

If someone were to ask you the question "What is your greatest need?" how would you answer? I suspect many answers to that question would revolve around finances, relationships, and life circumstances. However, the Bible is adamant that none of these are our greatest need. Whether we are cognizant of it or not, **our greatest need according to the Bible is the forgiveness of our sins!** Jesus dying on a cross for our sins, the premise of Christianity, only makes sense when we understand that forgiveness is our greatest need.

A Christian perspective of sin involves understanding three other Biblical truths.

#1- Sin is Both an Act and a Condition.

The Bible also uses the term "sin" to describe both our acts and condition. Telling a lie would be an act of sin, but the reason we tell lies is because we suffer from the condition of sin.

We sin because we have a sin nature – a propensity towards sin. To state it in theological terms, we sin because we are sinners, we are not sinners because we sin. In the confessional of the 51st Psalm we find both the act and the condition of sin alluded to by Israel's King David. He prays about his act of sin saying "cleanse me from my sin" and comments about his condition of sin "surely I was sinful at birth, in sin did my mother conceive me." Because of our condition the Bible uses the words "lost", "blind", and even "dead" to describe our spiritual state before God.

#2- God is Holy

Sin is very serious to a HOLY God. Holy means "set apart" or "separate from sin". Because of God's holiness even one sin is enough to keep us separated from him ..... "You who are of purer eyes than to see evil and cannot look at wrong" (Habakkuk 1:13 ESV). Because of God's holiness sin cannot go unpunished. "He does not leave the guilty unpunished" (Numbers 14:18 NIV). Because of God's holiness even our best deeds fall short.... "even our best deeds are as filthy rags". Hell, a place of eternal separation from God, exists because of God's holiness.

#3- All Sin is against God.

Perhaps the most important and least recognized Biblical perspective of sin is that ultimately all sin is against God. God is our Creator and we were created by Him and for Him. At it's essence sin is not living as God intends. Therefore, every sin is against Him even when it might involve other people. We see this illustrated over and over in the Bible. Joseph when given the opportunity to sleep with another man's wife said. 'How then can I do this great wickedness and sin against God?' (Genesis 39:9).We find in the Proverbs that "whoever mocks the poor insults his Maker" Proverbs 17:5. In the book of Acts, when Ananias and Sapphira lie to the apostles, Peter says to them "You have not lied just to human beings but to God." When we understand our sin from this perspective it enables us to understand it's seriousness. Here is a graphic illustration to illuminate this point.

"If you were to discover a little boy pulling the legs off of a grasshopper, you would think it strange and perhaps a little bizarre. If the same little boy were pulling the legs off of a frog, that would be a bit more disturbing. If it were a bird, you would probably scold him and inform his parents. If it were a puppy, that would be too shocking to tolerate. You would intervene. If it were a little baby, it would be so reprehensible and tragic that you would risk you own life to protect the baby. What's the difference in each of these scenarios? The sin is the same (pulling the limbs off). The only difference is the one sinned against (from a grasshopper to a baby). The more noble and valuable the creature, the more heinous and reprehensible the sin."[1]

When we come to understand that sin is both an act and condition, God is holy, and all sin is against God we come understand that we are in a dire situation. This perspective helps us to understand why Christ came. Many people mistakenly think Christ came primarily to communicate his love for us. While indeed he does love us (John 3:16), he primarily came to rescue us. A common illustration I use to clarify this truth is to compare a couple of different scenarios involving my wife and myself. [2]

Scenario #1- My wife and I are out on a ship by ourselves in the middle of the ocean. I say to my wife "I Love You" and "to communicate my love for you I am going to jump overboard and drown myself… that way you will know I love you". Knowing my wife the way that I do, her response would be "That is the stupidest thing I have ever heard."

Scenario #2 – My wife and I are out on a ship by ourselves in the middle of the ocean. The ship springs a leak and begins to sink. We make an SOS call and the rescuers are not going to make it to us in time. On the ship is one life preserver and I give it to my wife to wear. I go down with ship in death and she is rescued.

Christianity is much more analogous to Scenario #2 than it is Scenario #1. Christ loves us and we know this because he came to rescue us. Christ came to take the punishment for our sins. Christ who never sinned became sin for us so that we might be made right with God. (2 Corinthians 5:21). Christ came to be "the atoning sacrifice for our sins." (I John 2:2). Christianity is experiencing the rescue of our souls. That experience comes through repentance and faith.

Notes:

1. Denny Burk, "Postscript on Hell" (dennyburk.com/postscript-on-hell/#more-13289, 13.jul.2011). Denny shares an illustration from Joe Blankenship, pastor of Springs of Grace Bible Church in Tulsa, Oklahoma.

2. Adapted from a sermon by Dr. Timothy Keller. (Dr. Keller's sermons are available online at itunes.apple.com/us/podcast/timothy-keller-podcast/id352660924).

3. Repentance

As I mentioned earlier becoming a Christian requires two essentials, repentance and faith. "Repent" was the first word uttered by Jesus as he began his earthly ministry. It was also the first word of John the Baptist's ministry and Peter's first sermon. I guess it goes without saying that it is an important word to understand from a Christian perspective.

Repentance means to change one's mind, to turn, or literally do a 180 degree turn. The visual is of a person going in one direction and doing a 180 turn around and walking in another direction. Repentance means to come to understand that you are walking away from God, which according to the Bible we are all doing. The Bible says that we have all sinned and fallen short of God's standard (Romans 3:23).

Repentance is an overall attitude towards sin, both as our condition and as individual acts. It involves our mind, our emotions, and our will. It is manifested in the mind by an acknowledgement of guilt. It is manifested in the emotions by a sorrowfulness over the sin. It is manifested in the will by a decision to turn from sin and change in behavior. True repentance involves the total person.

My favorite description of repentance is found in the story of the prodigal son in Luke 15.

" Jesus continued: "There was a man who had two sons. 12 The younger one said to his father, 'Father, give me my share of the estate.' So he divided his property between them.13 "Not long after that, the younger son got together all he had, set off for a distant country and there squandered his wealth in wild living. 14 After he had spent everything, there was a severe famine in that whole country, and he began to be in need. 15 So he went and hired himself out to a citizen of that country, who sent him to his fields to feed pigs. 16 He longed to fill his stomach with the pods that the pigs were eating, but no one gave him anything.17 "When he came to his senses, he said, 'How many of my father's hired servants have food to spare, and here I am starving to death! 18 I will set out and go back to my father and say to him: Father, I have sinned against heaven and against you. 19 I am no longer worthy to be called

your son; make me like one of your hired servants.'
[20] So he got up and went to his father. "But while he
was still a long way off, his father saw him and was
filled with compassion for him; he ran to his son,
threw his arms around him and kissed him. [21] "The
son said to him, 'Father, I have sinned against
heaven and against you. I am no longer worthy to be
called your son.' [22] "But the father said to his
servants, 'Quick! Bring the best robe and put it on
him. Put a ring on his finger and sandals on his feet.
[23] Bring the fattened calf and kill it. Let's have a feast
and celebrate. [24] For this son of mine was dead and is
alive again; he was lost and is found.' So they began
to celebrate Luke 15: 11 - 23

The father in this story is an obvious metaphor
of our Heavenly Father. This story helps us
understand that sin is not just "the breaking of a
rule" to God. Sin is personal, relational, and
heartbreaking to God. It is also an obvious
metaphor for repentance and we see how
repentance involves the whole person. We see
the prodigal's mind involved "he came to his
senses," his will involved "he got up and went
to his father", and his emotions involved
'Father, I have sinned against heaven and
against you. I am no longer worthy to be called
your son.' Repentance for the prodigal son
involved his total person and so it must for us

as well. A truly repentant person comes to understand and acknowledges their guilt before God (mind), experiences sorrow over their sin (emotions), and crosses that invisible line in their hearts to turn from sin (will). **Repentance means Christ becomes the Leader of your life.**

4. Faith

Faith is the other essential in becoming a Christian. The Bible says in Ephesians 2:8-9 that we are "**saved** by grace **through faith**, not by works." Faith is trust or total dependence in Christ and his death for the forgiveness of our sins. He becomes the Forgiver of our life.

It is crucial to understand the relationship between faith and works in order to have a correct understanding of Christianity. This is where Christianity distinguishes itself from other religions. Being a good person, having your good outweigh your bad, or doing good things does not get a person into heaven. Christianity doesn't teach good people go to heaven, it teaches no one is good. Christ's death was necessary because none of us could be good enough – "there is no one good, no not one" (Romans 3: 10). This is not to say that good works don't matter. The Bible says in Ephesians 2:10 that "we were created in Christ Jesus for good works" In other words works will accompany someone who has faith, but it is not faith. Faith alone saves, but saving faith is not alone. A person who is trusting Christ alone for salvation will have a life accompanied by works showing their faith is sincere. Faith comes first, and along comes works.

Another way to understand faith is to say it this way, "All other religions are spelled DO, but Christianity is spelled DONE." It is about what Christ has DONE for us on the cross and appropriating or applying his death to our life. Faith is trusting in Christ and his death alone for the forgiveness of our sins. **Faith is Christ becoming the Forgiver of one's life.**

The Bible also uses the word "believe" to describe faith. Perhaps the most famous verse in the Bible John 3:16 says "whoever believes in Him (Jesus) will not perish, but have everlasting life." Another clear statement about the need for faith where the Bible uses the word "believe" is Acts 16:32 "Believe in the Lord Jesus, and you will be saved."

It is important to know that belief in the Bible involved more than just believing something at a cognitive level or intellectual assent. In other words it is belief not only with the head, but with the heart. For years prior to my own Christian conversion I "believed" in Jesus, but it was not the kind of "believe" that the Bible describes. Like repentance, faith (believing) involves the whole person and includes the mind, emotions, and will. **Real believing manifests itself as commitment to Christ**.

One of the popular "preacher stories" that is told to illustrate faith is that of the Niagara Falls tightrope walker.

One day long ago, a world-renowned tightrope walker came to Niagara Falls and stretched his rope across the thunderous currents from the United States to Canada. Right before the eyes of the breathless crowds, he walked, ran, even tiptoed across the chasm. As he came back to the other side he asked the crowds, how many of you believe I can do this blindfolded Many waved their hands in the air and shouted I do I believe. As he completed the feat he can back to the crowd and asked How many of you think I can do this blindfolded? He did the same blindfolded. Then, still blindfolded, he pushed a wheelbarrow across the falls. The crowd went wild when the aerialist shouted, "Who believes

I can push a man in this wheelbarrow across these falls?" One rather enthusiastic gentleman in the front of the crowd waved his hand in the air, shouting, "I do! I believe!" "Then," said the tightrope walker, "climb on in!" Needless to say, the once eager spectator dropped his hand and slinked back into the crowd. His intellectual assent didn't quite translate into personal faith. He did not really "believe."

Ultimately faith is manifested by commitment. Real saving faith involves the total person and total commitment. Christ becomes the Forgiver and Leader of one's life.

5. The Change

Sad but true, I was extremely vain when I was a young kid. This especially became problematic when it was discovered that I was near sighted and needed glasses. I didn't want glasses because I was afraid of what I would look like and the other kids might call me "four eyes." Eventually it became obvious though that I could not go without glasses and I gave in to getting glasses.

I will always vividly remember the day I picked up that first pair of glasses. I sat down across from the technician and she had me try on the glasses to make sure that they fit. I put on the pair of glasses and turned to look out the window amazed at how clear everything looked in the distance. I remember saying to the young woman "The windows are not dirty." Up until that moment, I had just assumed that I could not see things clearly in the distance when looking out the window because the windows were dirty. I now saw life differently.

This childhood memory somewhat serves as a spiritual analogy to what happened to me and anyone when they truly repent of their sins and put their faith in Christ. A person comes to understand their spiritual blindness and puts on spiritual eyesight (Christ); therefore, seeing life differently. As 1 Corinthians 5:17 states, "If anyone is in Christ, they are a new creation, the old has passed away the new has come." Jesus also used phrases like "born again" and "converted" to describe what happens when one becomes a Christian.

Other places in the Bible use metaphors such as going from "darkness to light", "blindness to sight", and from "death to life" to describe what happens. **To put it in plain and simple terms, a person who has truly become a Christian is changed.** The Bible attributes this change to the work and indwelling of the Holy Spirit. The Bible describes it this way in Ephesians 1:13: "In him (Christ) you also, when you heard the word of truth, the gospel of your salvation, and believed in him, were sealed with the promised Holy Spirit." This change is dramatic in varying degrees and differs from person to person. For those living an irreligious / immoral life it is a dramatic change in behavior. For those living a religious / moral life, it is a dramatic change in motives for behavior. This change for some can almost be instantaneous, but for others occur over a period of time. Some Christians can remember the exact moment and time they became a Christian, but others recall a period of time characterized by repentance and faith. Whether is was instantaneous or over a period of time a Christian is someone who NOW has Christ as the Forgiver and Leader of their life.

This change is how one knows they are a Christian. Along with a moment in time of responding with the essentials of repentance and faith comes evidence of its sincerity. This evidence is most notable in one's attitude towards sin. The Bible describes it like this in 1 John 3:9, "No one born of God makes a practice of sinning, for God's seed abides in him, and he cannot keep on sinning because he has been born of God." A person who has truly becomes a Christian will live a lifestyle of striving to obey God. That is not to say a true Christian will never sin, but their lives will be characterized by a turning from sin and turning to Christ for forgiveness. This obedience is not to earn God's acceptance, but because they have been accepted by God through Christ. A person can know they are a Christian because they have responded to God in repentance and faith and their lives are now evidenced by a present and continuing response to Christ as Forgiver and Leader of their life.

6. Assurance

Everyone who reads this book falls into one of these four categories regarding assurance of their salvation, or knowing they are truly a Christian.

Category #1- Someone who is truly a Christian and knows it. *(ASSURANCE)*

Category #2- Someone who thinks they are truly a Christian, but is **NOT.** *(FALSE ASSURANCE)*

Category #3- Someone who is truly a Christian, but does not know it. *(LACKS ASSURANCE)*

Category #4- Someone who is NOT a Christian and knows it. *(NO ASSURANCE)*

To state the obvious, my hope would be that everyone after reading this book would belong to Category #1. **God's will is for someone to**

have assurance about their eternity.
Assurance comes through having an
understanding of how one becomes and a
Christian and then examining ourselves to see
if we have done what is required. The Bible
says it this way "Test yourselves to see if you
are in the faith; examine yourselves! Or do you
not recognize this about yourselves, that Jesus
Christ is in you - unless indeed you fail the
test?" (2 Corinthians 13:5). We are to "test"
ourselves. This test can basically be summed
up in two questions.

Question #1- Has there been a time in my life
when I recognized my need for Christ and
repented of my sin and put my faith in Christ?

Question #2- Since that time and presently is
my life characterized by a turning from sin and
living for Christ?

To pass the test, to have assurance, you must
answer YES to both questions. If you can
answer yes to both of these questions God
wants you to know that "you have eternal life"
(1 John 5:13 ESV). Without exaggeration, this
test is the most important one anyone can ever
take....eternity with or without God is at stake.

My hope and prayer is that everyone who reads this book would take some time to sincerely consider these two questions after first asking God in prayer to help you answer them honestly.

At 20 years of age I came to understand Christianity and sincerely ask myself these two questions. After some serious introspection I knew that I failed the test. I responded in my heart with repentance and faith along with a simple prayer, "Save me!" I know that he answered that prayer because the Bible says "For everyone who calls on the name of the Lord will be saved" (Romans 10:13 ESV).

If you cannot answer YES to these two questions I hope that you will make a decision today to repent of your sin and put your faith in Christ. I think it is best to seal your decision of repentance and faith in a prayer. There are no right or wrong words to pray but I would suggest:

"God I know that I am a sinner and separated from you. I ask you to forgive my sin. I repent of my sin and put my faith in Christ. I want Christ as the Forgiver and Leader of my life. Save Me!"

7. Next Steps

God's will for our lives it to know him through a relationship with Christ and to grow in that relationship with Him. Just as there are essentials to entering into a relationship with God (repentance and faith), there is also essentials to growing in a relationship with God. Though not a conclusive list, let me mention four:

#1- Bible Reading

#2- Prayer

#3- Church

#4- Baptism

Bible Reading

Jesus said, "People do not live by bread alone, but by every word that comes from the mouth of God" (Matthew 4:4 NLT). The Bible is

God's word to us. It is how God speaks to us, relates to us, and changes us. Reading and applying the Bible daily to our lives is essential.

Prayer

The Bibles says that "Jesus often withdrew to lonely places and prayed" (Luke 5:16 NIV). We also find him praying not only by himself but with his disciples "he took with him Peter and John and James and went up on the mountain to pray" (Luke 9:20 ESV). Prayer is simply talking to and listening to God. Along with the Bible, prayer is a daily essential for growing in our relationship with God.

Church

Christian growth happens in community, in a church family. The writer of the biblical book of Hebrews says, "Let us not give up meeting together ... let us encourage one another" (Hebrews 10:25). It is of utmost importance to find a Bible-believing church (one that believes and teaches the Bible) to plug into.

Baptism

There is disagreement over the mode, timing, and meaning of baptism within Christianity. But all would agree that baptism is an important part and should be done when a person is a Christian. For the record, my personal view of baptism is that it should be done after a person becomes a Christian as a public profession of Christ. Acts 2:38 says "Repent and be baptized, every one of you, in the name of Jesus Christ for the forgiveness of your sins."

If you have read this far, I really hope I have accomplished my goal of helping you in *Understanding Christianity* and you now know "what it means to become a Christian." **My ultimate hope and prayer is that if you are not a Christian, you will become one!** Perhaps a fitting verse to close is 2 Corinthians 6:2, "Behold, now is the acceptable time, behold, now is the day of salvation" (NASB).

May God use this book to be "the day of salvation" for many!!

God Bless,

Brent

About

Brent Devenney is Lead Pastor of Daybreak Community Church in Colchester, VT. Along with being a pastor for the past twenty years, he has worked as an oncology RN in a variety of settings. Brent and his wife, Lori, reside in South Burlington, VT, and have three children.

Suggested Sinner's Prayer

- *"God I know that I am a sinner and separated from you. I ask you to forgive my sin. I repent of my sin and put my faith in Christ. I want Christ as the Forgiver and Leader of my life. Save me!"*

"For 'everyone who calls on the name of the Lord will be saved.'" (Romans 10:13 ESV).